LINDA MO\

C000170708

CASSAVA AND CHICHA
Bread and Beer
of the Amazonian Indians

SHIRE ETHNOGRAPHY

Cover photograph
Two Tiriyo women grating manioc into a trough.
(Photographed in Surinam by Dr Peter Rivière of the Institute of Social Anthropology, Oxford.)

British Library Cataloguing in Publication Data:
Mowat, Linda.
Cassava and chicha: bread and beer of the Amazonian Indians.
— (Shire Ethnography; 11).
1. Brazil. Amazon River Basin
South American Indians. Social life, history.
I. Title.
981'. 100498.
ISBN 0-7478-0008-1.

Dedicated to the memory of Bryan Cranstone, whose fascination with ethnography has done so much to promote the study of other cultures.

Published by
SHIRE PUBLICATIONS LTD
Cromwell House, Church Street, Princes Risborough,
Aylesbury, Bucks HP17 9AJ, UK.

Series Editor: the late Bryan Cranstone

Copyright: Linda Mowat, 1989.
All rights reserved.
No part of this publication may be reproduced or transmitted in any form or by any means, electronic or mechanical, including photocopy, recording, or any information storage and retrieval system, without permission in writing from the publishers.

ISBN 0 7478 0008 1

First published 1989.

Printed in Great Britain by
C. I. Thomas & Sons (Haverfordwest) Ltd,
Press Buildings, Merlins Bridge, Haverfordwest, Dyfed SA61 1XF.

Contents

Acknowledgements

I would like to thank Peter Rivière and Donald Tayler for permission to use their field photographs and for their valuable comments on the text; also Malcolm Osman for his assistance with the photography. I am indebted to the staff of the Museum of Mankind, Horniman Museum and Cambridge University Museum of Archaeology and Anthropology for their assistance with my research and for permission to reproduce photographs. Most of all I am grateful to my husband David for his enthusiasm and support.

4

List of illustrations

1
Introduction

Most of the indigenous people of the tropical forests and savannahs of South America depend for their subsistence on a tuberous plant called manioc. From manioc they make bread known as cassava, a kind of toasted flour called farinha and a variety of beers coming under the generic name of chicha. Manioc is also extensively used by the Maroons of Surinam (descendants of escaped African slaves) and in the West Indies, where it was originally cultivated by the Arawaks and Caribs.

The tropical forest Indians have an economic tradition based on hunting, fishing, collecting and gardening in varying proportions. Some groups do not cultivate at all; for others horticulture is their major source of food. Some are sedentary and permanently settled, usually in a riverine environment; others shift their base of operations more or less often in their quest for food. The traditional settlement is based on large communal houses for extended families; one or more of these may constitute a village. Social organisation tends to be informal with no established hierarchy, authority resting in the hands of the household heads.

Cultural similarity over the huge area of the tropical forest, which spans much of Brazil, the Guianas, Venezuela, Colombia, Ecuador, Peru and Bolivia, is such that it is possible to make broad generalisations regarding manioc horticulture and the production of cassava and chicha. However, it should be realised that there are exceptions to every rule and that no two groups are likely to work in exactly the same way.

Work on any aspect of South American Indian culture must take into account the changes currently being undergone by the people concerned. There are today virtually no uncontacted tribes in Amazonia, and it is rare to find any group living entirely according to its cultural traditions without white influence. The effects of social, economic and environmental change will be considered throughout the text, and especially in chapter 6.

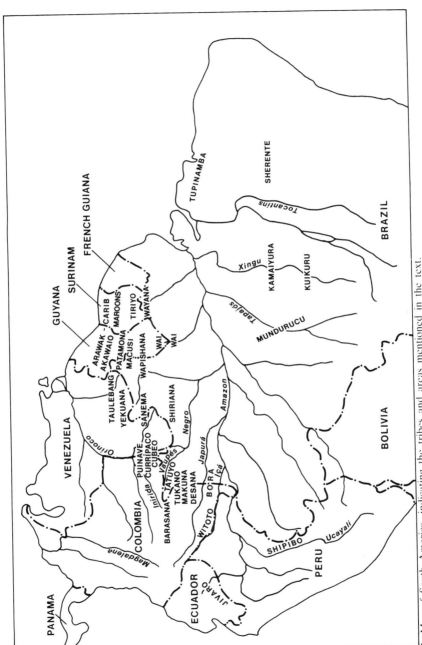

1. Map of South America, indicating the tribes and areas mentioned in the text.

2
The manioc plant

Manioc (*Manihot esculenta*) is known as *mandioca* in Brazil and Paraguay, and *yuca* in most parts of Spanish America. It is also commonly referred to as cassava, although this is more correctly the term for the flat round cakes of bread made from manioc flour.

Manioc is a perennial shrub with umbrella-shaped leaves and starchy storage roots (figure 2). It grows to a height of about 6-9 feet (1.80-2.70 metres), and the tubers on harvesting may be 1-2 feet (300-600 mm) long. There are numerous varieties of manioc which differ in terms of the height and appearance of the shrub as well as the colour and starch content of the tuber.

Manioc has traditionally been divided into two main types: sweet and bitter. Sweet manioc tubers may be simply baked or boiled and eaten as a vegetable; bitter manioc, on the other hand, is toxic and needs elaborate processing to make it edible. It is now established that sweet and bitter manioc belong to the same species, but their nature depends on the quantity of cyanogenic glucosides present in the tubers. These glucosides break down on exposure to air to form hydrocyanic (prussic) acid, which is highly poisonous. Varieties with a low glucoside content are termed sweet; those with a high glucoside content are termed bitter.

Manioc is native to the tropical forests of South America, though its area of origin is a matter of some dispute. Suggestions by scholars are based on the current distribution of wild species of the genus *Manihot*, and include Mexico, the shores of the Caribbean, north-eastern Brazil, the Magdalena-Sinú basin of Colombia and the Orinoco Basin of Colombia/Venezuela. Manioc is well suited to upland humid tropical environments, and needs alternate wet and dry seasons to grow successfully. Although it is sometimes grown in association with maize, maize is better suited to clayey river-bottom soils with plenty of nutrients.

Sweet manioc has a wider distribution than bitter and is much easier to convert into food. However, where available, bitter manioc has frequently been preferred as a staple crop by tropical forest Indians. It has a higher starch content and is more suitable for making flour and bread. (While sweet manioc may be used for this purpose, the bread will not keep very long.) A great deal of experimentation must have taken place in the early stages of

2. Manioc growing in a Tiriyo garden, Surinam. (Copyright: Peter Rivière.)

manioc cultivation to master the art of detoxification, but the end product has long been regarded as worth the hard work involved. This book is mostly concerned with bitter manioc.

The nutritional value of bitter manioc lies mainly in its starch content: it produces millions more calories per hectare than maize, the principal South American cereal crop. However, it has only 0.5 per cent fat, and the protein content is very low — about 1.7 per cent as opposed to 7 per cent for cereal crops. This protein is of poor quality and in areas where manioc is the staple it is necessary to supplement the diet with meat and fish, or the protein deficiency disease kwashiorkor will develop in children. Indian groups depending on manioc traditionally obtain protein from hunting, fishing and gathering.

Manioc has been cultivated for thousands of years in South America and the West Indies, the earliest evidence dating from about 2000 BC in the Orinoco basin. However, it is not easy to identify manioc in the archaeological record. Cereal crops can be recognised by carbonised grains from hearths or middens, but manioc, dependent on vegetative reproduction, leaves no seeds which could be preserved by burning. Some plants are identifiable by the pollen grains they leave behind, but in manioc the flowering and seed producing organs are so weak that scarcely any pollen is produced. The possibility of whole tubers surviving in the humid environment of the tropical forest is remote.

It is therefore usually necessary to rely on indirect evidence for manioc cultivation. This may take the form of fragments of the stone or pottery griddles on which cassava was baked (figure 3), or quantities of the minute stone chips which are all that survive of ancient manioc graters. While it is possible that such artefacts were used for processing other crops, their similarity to recent examples of manioc equipment is striking. In addition, they tend to occur on sites with no evidence for maize production, suggesting that manioc was the staple crop in these locations.

Since the conquest of Central and South America by the Spanish and Portuguese, manioc as a staple has spread to the Old World as well as the New. It is now a major crop in much of tropical Africa and significant in parts of South-east Asia, Indonesia and Oceania. As it cannot tolerate frost, it will not grow in temperate climates.

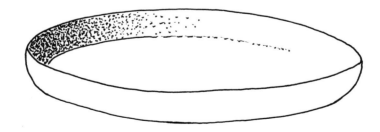

3. Common form of pottery manioc griddle found in archaeological deposits.

4. Tiriyo man with machete, Surinam. (Copyright: Peter Rivière.)

3
Cultivation

Manioc is traditionally grown in garden plots cleared in the tropical forest. These gardens are often referred to as *chagras* or *conucos*.

Tropical forest soils are not very fertile. Intensive weathering of the bedrock over long periods results in deep soils from which most of the nutrients, such as nitrogen, have been leached or washed away by abundant rainfall. Most nutrients are in fact held in the forest vegetation rather than in the soil and if they are to be utilised for agriculture the vegetation has to be cut and burned. The ash will then fertilise the soil for a few years, after which it will be necessary to make another clearing. This system is known as 'slash-and-burn' or 'swidden' cultivation. Abandoned gardens are left to lie fallow, sometimes for twenty years or more, while the natural vegetation takes over again in the form of secondary forest. In its traditional application to small-scale shifting horticulture, swidden cultivation does not disrupt the ecological balance of the forest.

Manioc is not very demanding of soil nutrients and a manioc plot will last longer than a maize plot before the soil is exhausted. The normal life of a garden is two to four years, representing two to three successive plantings. Manioc produces a high yield per hectare and needs less rainfall than maize. It also protects the soil from leaching to a certain extent: the umbrella leaves shield the ground from rain and help to keep temperatures low. This counteracts the effect of clearing, which raises temperatures and speeds up the decay of humus.

Manioc needs well drained soil, for waterlogging will destroy the tubers. It therefore cannot be planted in areas subject to periodic flooding, such as river banks. On the other hand it survives drought well, and may drop its leaves to reduce transpiration of moisture. Its long feeder roots can reach deep soil moisture, while the tubers store enough starch and water to re-establish the leaves when the drought is over.

Preparing the gardens

Seasons are by no means uniform throughout the tropical forest of South America. While one area may have one dry and one wet season every year, another may have two dry seasons alternating with two wet. Similarly, whereas in one area a dry

season will be completely dry, in another it may be only relatively
so compared with the wet season. Rainfall may vary from year to
year, and drought is often a risk. Cultivators have to adjust
themselves to the peculiarities of their particular environment.

Clearing of gardens is usually done at the end of a wet season,
thus giving the fallen trees and brush a few months to dry out
before they are burned. Clearing is invariably done by men,
either singly or communally, depending on the custom of the
group in question. When a new house is built the manioc gardens
will be close to it, but once these plots are exhausted it is
necessary to move cultivation further into the forest.

A man will try to select a plot with soft, well drained soil
containing plenty of organic material. He may clear a new garden
adjacent to one already in use or he may regard the danger from
predators to be less if the plots are spaced out. Once the distance
from house to garden becomes uneconomic in terms of travelling
time, the house may have to be relocated. However, in areas
where populations are sedentary, sometimes due to the proximity
of towns, trading-posts or mission-stations, gardens are often
situated at a considerable distance from settlements. In such cases
temporary camps may be constructed near the gardens for
occupation during intensive periods of work.

After marking out the plot by slashing the trunks of peripheral
trees, the first task is to cut the underbrush. This is done with a
steel machete (figure 4), an all-purpose cutlass traded from the
white man. Cutting brush can involve a great deal of work,

5. 'Machete' of chonta palm wood, Jivaro Indians, Ecuador. (Pitt Rivers Museum, Oxford.)

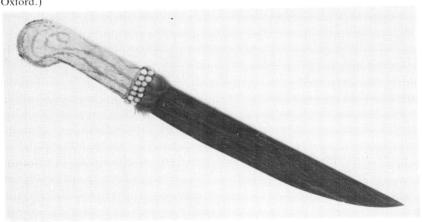

6. Tiriyo man cutting down tree with steel axe, Surinam. (Copyright: Peter Rivière.)

especially if secondary forest is being cleared. Prior to the availability of the machete, the Kuikuru of the Upper Xingu River in Brazil would use half a piranha mandible for this purpose; hardwood slashers have also been recorded (figure 5).

Next the trees are felled, using a steel axe also obtained from trade (figure 6). Previously stone axes (figure 7) were used for this work, which must have been extremely laborious. Stone axes rapidly become dull and need constant sharpening to remain effective. Nowadays old stone axes, if found, may be used by the Indians as whetstones for their steel tools.

Small trees and saplings are cut straight through with the steel axe. If the plot is on a slope, which it often is so that the soil will

7. (Above) Hafted stone axe, South America. (Right) Stone axe blade, Tocantins River, Brazil. (Pitt Rivers Museum, Oxford.)

drain, medium-sized trees are cut through halfway on the uphill side and a larger tree above then cut right through so as to topple a whole row of them with its weight. Very large trees may be girdled: the bark is cut through all round the tree and it is left to die. This was done more frequently before the advent of steel axes. Huge trees with buttress roots may necessitate the building of a scaffold to enable the trunk to be cut above the roots.

The cleared brush and fallen trees are left to dry out for a period and burned towards the end of the dry season. Burning should ideally take place on a dry sunny day with plenty of wind to help spread the fire through the garden. If the trunks are still damp, perhaps because the 'dry season' was not completely dry, burning can be a long and arduous business. On the other hand a garden of dry brush and wood can be burned in a couple of hours.

A newly burned garden is a jumbled mess of ashes and partly consumed trunks and stumps. It may be tidied up to a certain extent, but in general planting is done around and among the obstacles.

Planting

After burning, Barasana men in Colombia ritually cool a garden plot with beeswax before the women take it over and start planting. While planting is often women's work, it may be communal and is occasionally undertaken by men only.

Planting normally takes place soon after burning, just before the rains are due to start, as the cuttings need plenty of moisture in order to germinate. The Spanish chronicler Oviedo, writing in the sixteenth century, reported that the Indians of Hispaniola (now Haiti and the Dominican Republic) always planted at the beginning of the lunar month, so that the crop might grow with the moon. The Puinave of the River Inirida in Colombia begin by setting certain magic plants in the centre of the garden to ensure a good manioc harvest.

The soil is heaped together into mounds, which help to conserve moisture. Nowadays this is usually done with iron hoes, but digging sticks or wooden spades were used in the past. Several manioc cuttings (lengths of stem from existing plants) are then inserted into each mound. Pointed wooden dibbles or digging sticks assist in the process. Sometimes the holes are made by men, while the women insert the cuttings.

Several varieties, including sweet manioc, may be planted in one plot. To the untrained eye sweet and bitter manioc plants look very similar, but Indian cultivators have no difficulty in telling them apart. The garden may also be shared with other plants such as sugar cane, bananas, plantains, chili peppers, yams, maize, squash, pineapples, cotton, beans or rice. Traditionally gardens were always mixed; the increasing emphasis on manioc is due to the production of surplus for trade in the form of farinha.

Maintenance of the garden

The main problem in garden maintenance is protecting it from predators. The Akawaio of Guyana seek protection for their manioc crops by placing 'cassava spirit stones' in their gardens. Peccaries (wild pigs) are particularly voracious: they move in large groups and can devastate a garden in a very short time, climbing over or burrowing under all but the strongest fences. Agoutis and deer can also cause damage, and leafcutter ants, particularly in the Guianas, are impressively destructive of manioc plants.

Weeding is a necessary activity to keep the natural vegetation at bay and this is done with traded hoes, machetes or simply bare hands. Weeding tends to be a woman's activity. Once a garden reaches its second or third year the surrounding vegetation will be encroaching strongly and attempts at weeding become more desultory. At this stage it is easier to clear a new garden than to attempt to control the weeds.

The Barasana have a myth about the presence of weeds in manioc gardens. The first garden was planted by a group of sisters, all of whom were varieties of manioc apart from two who were weeds. The sister in charge told her husband not to watch the planting and ordered the manioc women to work in the centre of the plot while the weed women had to stay on the edge. However, her husband spied on the proceedings and in the resulting confusion weeds entered the manioc garden where they have been ever since.

Tropical forest women tend to be skilled cultivators, who take pride in their gardens and horticultural produce. They know the nutritional and breadmaking qualities of the different varieties of manioc and will experiment with unfamiliar strains. However, they are often unaware of fertilisers apart from the initial introduction of ash after burning the plot.

Harvesting

Manioc tubers mature in about eight months and may be harvested at this stage. However, a great advantage of manioc is that it can be stored in the ground and tubers can be left for up to two years without spoiling. After this time they become woody and cease to produce starch. The optimum time for harvesting is after about 20-22 months, by which time they have reached a size of up to 2 feet (600 mm) in length. If several gardens are kept with the manioc at different stages, the long maturing period provides a kind of insurance policy: if last year's crop is destroyed by predators, the latest planting can be harvested earlier than planned.

Harvesting is normally done by women, singly or in groups (figure 8). A woman will often take her daughter along to the garden as an assistant and chaperone. Occasionally, as in the case

8. Tiriyo woman harvesting manioc tubers, Surinam. (Copyright: Peter Rivière.)

of the Wai Wai of Guyana, men help with the harvest. As harvesting does not have to be done all at once, it may be virtually a daily activity, enough tubers being dug each day for that day's food. However, the frequency of harvesting depends on the custom of the group and the size of a woman's family. One estimate for the Puinave claims that 99 lbs (45 kg) of tubers will provide enough cassava for two adults and three children for a week.

Digging sticks and machetes are used to uproot the tubers. The plant stalks are not all discarded but cut to a suitable length, about 8-16 inches (200-400 mm), and stacked up for replanting, which may take place at intervals of several days. Replanting occurs two to three times during the life of a garden (figure 9).

The tubers may be scraped on the spot as this reduces the weight to be carried back to the house. They are then loaded into a carrying basket for transport home. These baskets vary in design, but often resemble a frame rucksack (figure 10, left), closed at the back with strips of fibre. Alternatively they may be cylindrical (figure 10, right). A tumpline of bast passes over the forehead, which takes the weight. Women carry loads of 50-75 lbs

Cassava and chicha

9. Tiriyo man planting manioc cuttings, Surinam. (Copyright: Peter Rivière.)

(23-34 kg) in such baskets, often over distances of several kilometres, and babies may be added to their cargo. Among the Desana of the Colombian North-west Amazon, a woman's carrying basket is burned at her death.

Although men make the manioc gardens, they are very much the domain of the women and may also be a refuge for them. Girls menstruating for the first time may undergo a period of isolation in the gardens; babies may be born there; and women may shelter there during male rituals they are not allowed to witness. Illicit lovemaking often takes place in the manioc

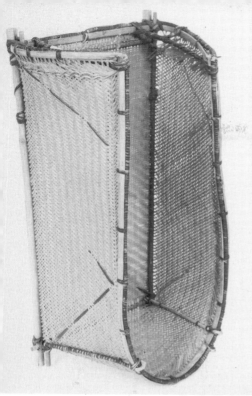

10. (Above) Carrying baskets. (Left) Akawaio Indians, Guyana. (Right) Sanema Indians, South Venezuela. (Pitt Rivers Museum, Oxford.)

11. (Right) Tiriyo women with carrying baskets, Surinam. (Copyright: Peter Rivière.)

gardens and marital sex there is said to have an extra degree of
excitement.

12. Tukano woman washing manioc tubers in the river, Colombia. (Copyright: B. Moser
and D. Tayler Collection.)

4
Processing

The processing of manioc may be done by each woman individually for her own family, perhaps with the aid of her daughter, daughter-in-law or sister, or it may be a communal affair for all the women of the house or village. The Mundurucú village comprises several women's and one men's house, with a special manioc-processing shed in the centre where women work together. Societies based on the communal house will have individual or shared facilities within it for working manioc.

Where women work together a hierarchy usually operates, with the most arduous jobs, such as grating, going to the youngest or to long-suffering daughters-in-law. In a few cases men may help with some steps of the work such as peeling, but this is uncommon. Men traditionally undertake the high-status tasks of hunting and fishing and generally regard it as beneath them to become involved in manioc processing.

The first stage is the peeling and washing of the tubers. Peeling may have been done in the garden, but it can be done after washing, which usually entails simply dumping a basket of tubers in the river and shaking it about (figure 12). Women usually wash themselves and their babies at the same time as the manioc. Peeling can then be done using a machete, a knife of steel, hardwood, cane or shell, a stone flake, or simply the teeth and fingers (figure 13). Tubers may be left to soak for some time before or after peeling: this helps to leach out the hydrocyanic acid. Either baskets are left in the river or the tubers are soaked in some large receptacle such as an old canoe.

Grating
Once the tubers are clean and peeled, the next stage is to grate them into a pulp. This must be done promptly as peeled tubers begin to deteriorate in a few hours. Perhaps the simplest method of grating is to rub the tubers on abrasive slabs of stone, for example granite or gneiss boulders found in the riverbeds. Lumps of coral may have been used for this in the West Indies: Oviedo wrote of *piedras asperas* (rough stones) being used to grate manioc there in the sixteenth century.

A much more sophisticated arrangement is the specially designed manioc grater (figure 14). This is usually a wooden board studded with minute chips of stone: quartz, flint, porphyry

13. Tukano woman peeling manioc tubers, Colombia. (Copyright: B. Moser and D. Tayler Collection.)

14. Manioc graters with stone teeth. (Above) Guyana. (Horniman Museum, London.) (Below right) Brazil. (Pitt Rivers Museum, Oxford). (Below left) North-west Amazon type, obtained from Macusi Indians, Guyana. (Museum of Mankind, London.)

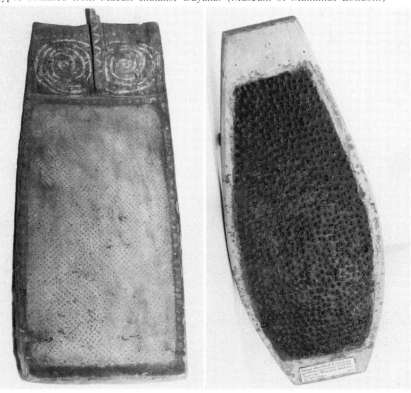

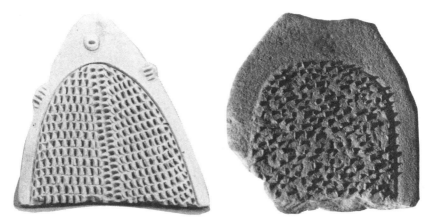

15. Ancient graters from Ecuador. (Left) Pottery. (Pitt Rivers Museum, Oxford.) (Right) Pottery with stone teeth. (Museum of Mankind, London.)

and granite have all been recorded. Indians would travel considerable distances to obtain the right kind of stone for graters.

Small graters of pottery, some in the shape of fish (or anthropomorphic fish) have been excavated from the Tumaco-La Tolita cultures of southern Colombia and Ecuador, dated from about 300 BC to AD 300 (figure 15). Some of these are set with stone teeth. It is possible that these were not made for practical use, but may have been linked with manioc rituals.

The manufacture of a manioc grater is usually a joint project between husband and wife. The man cuts the board and trims it to shape: in the Guianas graters tend to be flat and rectangular, whereas in the north-west Amazon they are concave and shield-shaped with a handle; waisted and trapezoidal forms are also found. Next either the man or the woman executes a design on it, then the woman chips the stone into tiny flakes and hammers them into the board, following the pattern (figure 16). The holes for the flakes were once made with a bone awl; nowadays an iron nail is more likely to be used for this purpose. An old iron tool or a wooden mallet may serve for hammering in the flakes.

When the Wai Wai manufacture graters no glue is used to secure the chips, but the finished grater is covered with a layer of red paint (made from the plant *Bixa orellana*) mixed with latex. This is claimed to be ornamental, but may help to keep the stones in place. Other tribes use tree gum, pitch, bird lime, vegetable glue or balata for this purpose. One report states that graters should be moistened before use to swell the wood and hold the chips in. Wai Wai men finish their graters with a design in black paint, made from leaf-ash, over the red. Some are even painted on the back (figure 17).

Stone-chip manioc graters were traditionally important items of intertribal trade, and were only made by certain groups of Indians. Graters of the Arawakan and Tukanoan tribes were particularly prized as trade objects and would be exchanged for such items as blowpipes, pottery, hammocks and hunting dogs. The Wai Wai traditionally traded their graters to the Wapishana, who did not make them. When the graters started to wear out, the Wapishana would pull out the valued stone chips and reset them.

Stone is by no means always available in the Amazon, and grating boards might also be manufactured with teeth of palm-wood, palm-thorns (figure 18), fish-bones or bone splinters. Thorny palm-roots could also be used, or even spiny fish-palates (figure 19). Nowadays graters with teeth of metal are often

16. Patterns of grater teeth. (Left) Stone teeth, Para, Brazil. (Right) Metal teeth, Yekuana Indians, Venezuela. (Museum of Mankind, London.)

preferred, a simpler version being a perforated sheet of tin, maybe part of an old oil can, sometimes wrapped around a block of wood. Copper graters were observed in Brazil as early as the mid nineteenth century. The latest invention is the mechanical grater, used by certain Indian groups in close contact with Europeans; it is worth noting that this labour-saving device involves the man in the domestic process: he turns the handle of the machine while his wife drops tubers into a hopper.

Manioc grating by the traditional method is an arduous and back-breaking job (figure 20). According to one report it took four women seven hours to grate 120 lbs (54 kg) of manioc. A woman will normally sit with her legs straight out and the grater braced between her abdomen and a house post. Then, grasping a tuber in each hand she grates back and forth vigorously with

17. Manioc grater, front and back, Wai Wai Indians, Guyana. (Horniman Museum, London.)

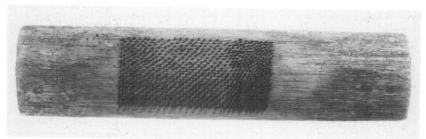

18. Bora manioc grater with teeth of palm-spines, Colombia. (Copyright: Cambridge University Museum of Archaeology and Anthropology.)

19. Fish-palate rasp for grating manioc, Brazil. (Pitt Rivers Museum, Oxford.)

alternate arm movements until the tubers are reduced to pulp, whereupon she takes up two more. Alternatively she may stand up to work, bending over the grater which is braced against her legs. Women may work together with their graters resting in a large wooden trough. This is the worst job in manioc processing and is generally delegated to the most junior members of the workforce.

The wet pulp may be placed in a purpose-built manioc trough, as among the Macusi, or in any convenient receptacle such as a basket, mat, palm-spathe or even an old canoe. It may at this stage be placed in a large round basketry sieve (figure 21) supported on a tripod and pounded with the fists until the liquid has all strained through the sieve. This helps to leach out the hydrocyanic acid, and is practised by the Tukano and the Wai Wai, among others. Water may be poured through the pulp to facilitate the process. Liquid from the pulp is collected in a pot beneath the sieve. It contains manioc starch, or tapioca, which eventually settles at the bottom of the pot. This may be

20. Tukano woman grating manioc, Colombia. (Copyright: B. Moser and D. Tayler Collection.)

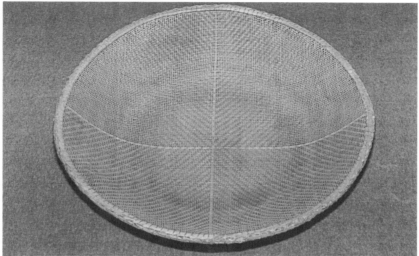

21. Sieve for pounding wet manioc pulp, Tukano Indians, Colombia. (Museum of Mankind, London.)

22. Manioc squeezer, Sherente Indians, Brazil. (Pitt Rivers Museum, Oxford.)

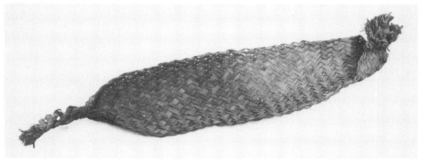

recombined with the pulp to make bread, or used separately (see below, section on squeezing).

Mundurucú women of the Tapajós River area of Brazil do not always grate their manioc tubers. When they are making a type of flour called *farinha d'agua* (water flour), they soak the tubers for three days, trample them in a trough, pick out the skins and then proceed directly to the squeezing process. The Tupinambá have a similar system. However, this process removes a lot of starch and the resulting flour is less nutritious than the more common

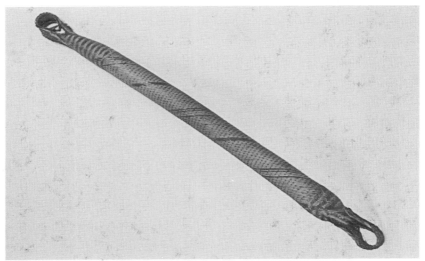

23. *Tipiti*, Akawaio Indians, Guyana. (Pitt Rivers Museum, Oxford.)

farinha seca (dry flour) made by grating fresh tubers. Yet another method involves soaking grated tubers for several weeks until they ferment and then squeezing. The Ica-Japurá tribes accelerate fermentation by adding some pieces of rotton manioc to the fresh tubers.

Squeezing
Squeezing helps to remove moisture from the grated manioc pulp. It has often been assumed that it is squeezing that eliminates the poisonous hydrocyanic acid from manioc, but in fact this is done by a permutation of soaking, washing, fermenting, drying, heating and cooking. Squeezing is therefore just one step in a complex overall process. The moisture pressed out of the pulp does, however, contain poisonous acid.

Pulp may be squeezed with the bare hands, or wrung in a strip of bark or a large leaf. Some tribes, for example the Witoto and Shirianá, twist a flexible mat tightly round the pulp. The Sherente also used this method (figure 22), which was later replaced with a piece of rag used in the same way. A plaited fibre sack open down one side is used to similar effect in certain areas. The Surinam Arawak used to put pulp in a fibre bag and squeeze it by sitting on a board placed on top. A conical basket called a *kamaiyo* was once used for the purpose in the Guianas.

The most ingenious and widespread method of squeezing manioc pulp is a flexible plaited basketry cylinder known as a *tipiti* or *matapi* (figure 23). It is referred to in Surinam as the 'Carib snake' and the term *culebra* or snake is fairly common for this artefact. There is a legend that the first Arawak man watched a snake swallowing its prey and made the first *tipiti* based on the movement of its body and the markings on its back.

The *tipiti*, made entirely of organic material, leaves no trace in the archaeological record. However, it may not be of great antiquity. It is found among tribes whose manioc horticulture is well developed, but has failed to reach groups on the headwaters of the Amazon to whom cultivation is less significant. As squeezing technology therefore appears to be in an evolutionary state, the *tipiti* may be a relatively recent invention.

The *tipiti* is plaited from reed stems, usually by men, and may be attractively patterned. Almost all basketry items are traditionally made by men in the tropical forest, using various types of reed, cane, vine, wood-splints and palm-leaves. The *tipiti* requires particular skill in its manufacture (figure 24): due to the diagonal plaiting the finished article may be stretched until it is long and thin, or contracted to make a short fat cylinder. The lower end is closed and there is a sturdy plaited loop at top and bottom. A *tipiti* may be up to 10 feet (3 metres) long. European screw-presses and lever-presses for manioc seem little more efficient than the *tipiti*, which has been extensively traded to the white man. The Taino (Arawak) people encountered in the West Indies by the *conquistadores* used a *tipiti* of woven cotton, the most evolved form in which it has been found.

In use the *tipiti* is pulled together to make it short and fat, and manioc pulp is stuffed into the cylinder, using the hands or a gourd spoon until, as Thomas Whiffen remarked in the early nineteenth century, 'it resembles nothing so much as a well filled Christmas stocking'. The top may be closed with a gourd to prevent overflowing of the pulp during squeezing. The upper loop is then hung from a peg driven into a house post. A pole is threaded through the lower loop and anchored at one end to the ground or the bottom of the house post. One or more women or children then sit on the free end of the pole, bouncing gently up and down, and their weight causes the *tipiti* to stretch and the juice from the pulp to be squeezed out (figure 25).

The poisonous juice is collected in a pot placed underneath the *tipiti* (figure 26). This may be of pottery (traditionally a women's craft), of gourd or, more commonly today, of aluminium.

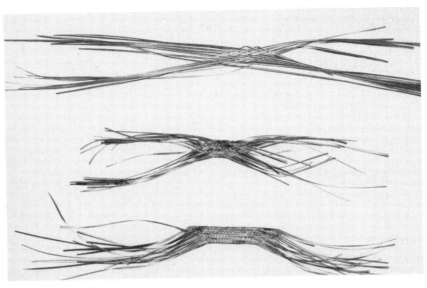

24. (Above, below and opposite) Sequence of *tipiti* manufacture, Guyana. (Museum of Mankind, London.)

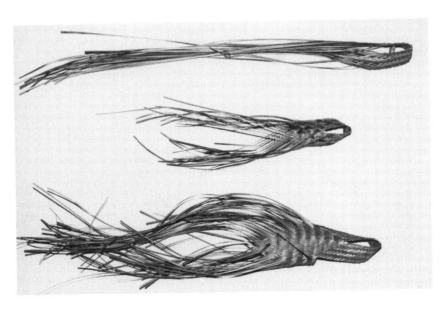

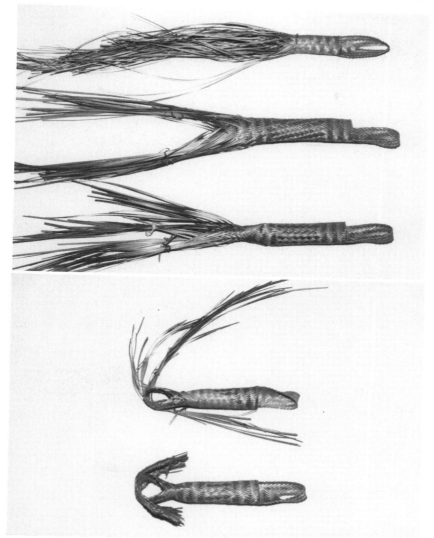

After some time pure white manioc starch (more universally known as tapioca) settles at the bottom of the pot and the poisonous juice may be poured off. Tapioca is valued for its whiteness and high nutritiousness. Barasana women used to put magical stones in the pot which they believed would increase the

25. Tiriyo woman using a *tipiti* to squeeze grated manioc pulp. Surinam. (Copyright: Peter Rivière.)

26. Pot for collecting juice and starch from the *tipiti*, Makuna Indians, Colombia. (Museum of Mankind, London.)

starch yield. Tapioca may be incorporated in ordinary cassava or made into various more elaborate forms of bread and manioc drinks. Among the Barasana tapioca bread, or 'starch cassava', is a special food eaten by girls in seclusion during their first menstruation and by boys undergoing initiation.

The poisonous juice is rarely thrown away. Most commonly it is boiled for several hours with chili peppers to make a thick savoury sauce which forms the basis of stew or 'pepper-pot'. Boiling drives off the hydrocyanic acid. This sauce is called *cassarip* in the Guianas and *tucupi* in Brazil. With cassava it forms the most basic type of meal. A small amount of *cassarip* and cassava will be offered to visitors to a village as a symbolic gesture of hospitality. *Cassarip* also forms the basis for stews with meat or fish. A thinner version, boiled for less time, may be consumed as a drink.

Sometimes manioc juice is utilised for its toxic qualities: the Wapishana and Macusi, for example, use it as a fish poison. The Wai Wai wash their dogs in it to rid them of their fleas, taking care to muzzle them to prevent them licking the juice before it has dried. Animals have been known to die after drinking raw manioc juice. Oviedo, writing in the sixteenth century of Indians reluctant to work for Spanish overlords in the West Indies, reports the drinking of manioc juice as an effective and immediate suicide method. Indeed whole groups of Indians

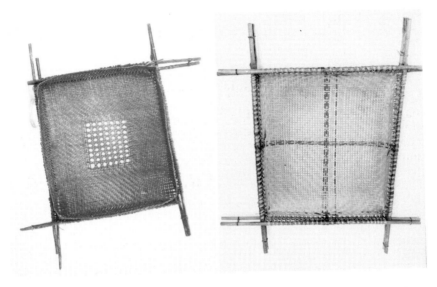

27. Manioc flour sieves. (Above left) Coarse sieve for farinha, Taulebang Indians, Venezuela. (Above right) Sieve for cassava flour, Akawaio Indians, Guyana. (Below left) Sieve for cassava flour, Tiriyo Indians, Surinam. (Below right) Sieve for cassava flour, Wayana Indians, Surinam (Pitt Rivers Museum, Oxford.)

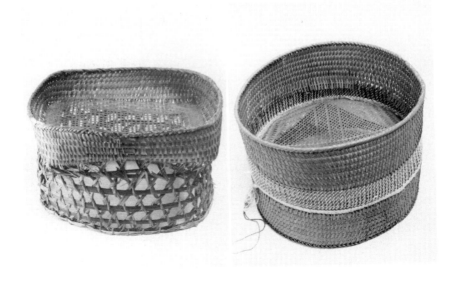

sometimes made pacts to kill themselves by this means. Eating raw tubers would have the same effect, but only after two or three days.

Baking

The squeezed manioc pulp is removed from the *tipiti* in compacted cylindrical sections and broken up with the hands. It may then be sieved immediately or subjected to further drying out, either in the sun or indoors on a shelf hung above the fire. This extra drying may take several days and also helps with the detoxification process. Once dry, the pulp may be pounded with a pestle and mortar before being rubbed through a basketry sieve. These may be round or rectangular and are of different grades depending on the quality of flour required (figure 27). Flour intended for cassava (bread) should be finer than that destined for farinha (coarse toasted flour). The residue in the sieve is either discarded or used for a coarse form of bread or a special beer.

Baking traditionally took place on a circular griddle of stone or pottery: often just a flat slab placed over the fire. Pottery griddles sometimes had rims to retain the flour. The griddle might be supported on three firedogs of pottery (figure 28) or simply on

28. Colombian pottery firedogs for supporting the manioc griddle. (Left) Taiwano Indians. (Right) Makuna Indians. (Museum of Mankind, London.)

29. Pottery manioc griddle, River Içana, Brazil. (After Koch-Grunberg 1909, 207.)

30. Stew-pots. (Above) Akawaio Indians, Guyana. (Pitt Rivers Museum, Oxford.) (Below) Patamona Indians, Guyana. (Horniman Museum, London.)

31. Tukano woman spreading flour on her griddle, Colombia. (Copyright: B. Moser and D. Tayler Collection.)

stones or lumps of clay. Some archaeological pottery griddles have built-in feet to support them; others have walls to contain the fire and are complete hearth units. Modern griddles from the north-west Amazon also incorporate walls (figure 29). Griddles have been reported up to 6 feet (1.83 metres) in diameter, though 2 feet 6 inches (760 mm) or less is a more usual size. Whiffen reported griddles of wood at the beginning of the twentieth

32. Tiriyo woman turning cassava with a fire-fan. Surinam. (Copyright: Peter Rivière.)

century though it is hard to understand how these would have withstood being placed on a fire.

Pottery artefacts are usually made by women in Amazonian societies, just as baskets are generally made by men. Plain pottery griddles require no great skill in the manufacture, being just flattened pancakes of clay left to dry out and then baked in an open fire. Archaeological griddles often bear impressions of the piece of cloth or matting on which they were made. As well as griddles, women would make stew-pots (often referred to as 'buck-pots' in the Guianas) (figure 30) and huge beer-pots, built up by coiling and requiring great skill. Decoration, particularly of beer pots, could be quite elaborate; alternatively pots could simply be blackened with manganese oxide, resin, plant juices or soot from old pots.

In the twentieth century pottery-making skills have declined, due to the availability of metal vessels through trade with Europeans. Pottery manioc griddles have also largely been replaced by metal ones (iron, or sometimes copper) which first became available towards the end of the eighteenth century. There are records of metal griddles being bartered for Indian slaves in Cayenne. In its simplest form a metal griddle is the end

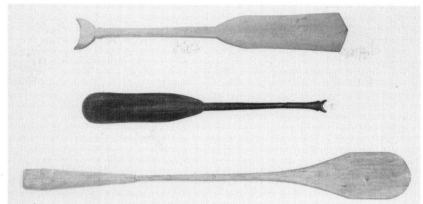

33. Wooden stirrers. (Upper and middle) Akawaio Indians, Guyana. (Lower) Wayana Indians, Surinam. (Pitt Rivers Museum, Oxford.)

34. Fire-fans. (Top left) Tiriyo Indians, Surinam. (Bottom left) Wayana Indians, Surinam. (Below) Akawaio Indians, Guyana. (Pitt Rivers Museum, Oxford.)

of an old oil can but purpose-built models are readily available, including pans with a retaining rim to hold in the flour. A pan with a rim is more convenient for making farinha.

The manioc griddle may be communal within the maloca, as among the Cubeo, or each wife may have her own. The griddle is heated over the fire before baking begins. Then flour is spread evenly over the hot surface, perhaps using a palm-spathe or a fire-fan as a scoop (figure 31). If cassava is being made (*cazabe* or *beiju* in Brazil) the grains are allowed to fuse together with the heat into a flat cake and turned after six to seven minutes to cook the other side (figure 32); for farinha the flour is stirred and toasted, keeping the grains separate. Various wooden stirrers may be used during baking (figure 33), and palm-leaf fans are particularly useful, not only for fanning the fire but as spatulas for turning farinha or cassava. Like nearly all basketry items they are usually made by men and may bear attractive designs (figure 34). There is an Arawak belief that if a woman used a fan on herself she would waste away. Cassava-smoothers may also be used and the Wai Wai have wooden cassava knives for trimming the edge of the cake. The Kamaiyura of the Upper Xingu River in Brazil use elaborate painted wood plaques for turning cassava (figure 35). The outside is not allowed to brown, and burned spots may be scraped off. The Wai Wai use a 'cassava-painter', a lump of tapioca, to whiten the surface of the bread. The cassava may be scored with a knife to make it easier to break into portions. The

35. Wooden plaque for turning cassava, Kamaiyura Indians, Brazil. (Pitt Rivers Museum, Oxford.)

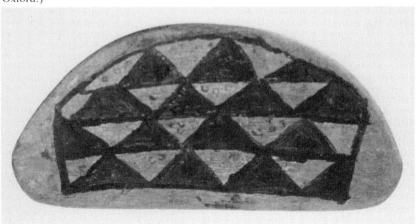

36. Cassava bread drying on roof of Tiriyo house, Surinam. (Copyright: Peter Rivière.)

Maroons of Surinam decorate cassava with finger-patterns which are baked into the cakes.

There are many different recipes for manioc bread, and each group will make several different kinds. Tapioca (the starch extracted from the squeezed manioc pulp), ground brazil nuts or fruits may be added to the basic flour in varying proportions to give breads of different flavours and textures, some of which are considered as delicacies and eaten on special occasions. Cassava to which tapioca has been added is very nutritious and of a stringy texture. Pure tapioca bread may also be made. Cassava flour may be subjected to different processes before baking, being sundried or smoked for varying periods. This helps to eliminate the hydrocyanic acid.

Cassava is often tossed upon the roof of the house to dry out in the sun prior to consumption or storage (figure 36). This makes it crisp. The Wayana of Brazil believe that cassava needs to be removed from the roof at midday, otherwise the sun will take it in its course and the manioc plants will die.

Storage

Once dry, cassava and farinha will keep for a very long time indeed, up to a year if necessary. Oviedo took some cassava to

37. Cassava serving trays. (Above) Sanema Indians, South Venezuela. (Below) Akawaio Indians, Guyana. (Pitt Rivers Museum, Oxford.)

Spain by sea in the sixteenth century, and it survived the lengthy voyage without deterioration. It is vital that it should be kept dry however, otherwise it will become mouldy, and protection from insects is also essential. Cassava and farinha are usually stored in baskets or on racks raised well above the ground. Baskets may be loosely-woven and lined with palm-leaves: these are also useful for transporting farinha. Large petrol cans may also be used as storage containers. While cassava and farinha can be kept for a considerable length of time, the fact that manioc tubers can be stored in the ground tends to render this unnecessary.

Serving

Cassava is usually served in round or square basketry trays, which may have intricate patterns woven into them (figure 37). Alternatively small mats or fire-fans may be used, or hour-glass shaped pot-stands. Pieces of bread are broken off with the fingers and dipped into a pot of sauce or stew before being eaten. Men and women do not normally eat together: a woman will serve her husband before having anything to eat herself.

Chicha

Chicha is the generic name applied to native beer in South America. It does not only apply to beverages fermented from sweet and bitter manioc, but also to those made from maize, sugar cane and various fruits. Similarly not all manioc beer is referred to as chicha, there being as many terms as there are recipes.

Not all manioc-based drinks are alcoholic. One of the simplest is made by boiling up the juice expressed from the *tipiti* to drive off the hydrocyanic acid and produce a sweetish, rather flavour-less beverage. A plain tapioca drink is produced by boiling manioc starch in water until thick, diluting with cold water and leaving to stand for a day. More flavoursome fruit drinks also involve manioc, the starch or flour being added to grated plantains, bananas and other fruits and boiled up to produce a thick nutritious liquid. If sugar cane is grown it may be combined with tapioca and water to make a sweet drink.

The recipes for manioc beer are many and various, but basically fermentation is induced either by masticating cassava and letting the enzymes in saliva do the work or by allowing mould to develop.

In the first method, cassava bread may be boiled or soaked in hot water, often with grated sweet potatoes, and mouthfuls of the mixture are chewed and spat back into the pot. The beverage is left to stand for a day or so before drinking. The *kachiri* of the Wayana and the *kurai* of the Wai Wai are made according to this method. Similarly, Guiana beers are based on a substance called *kereli*, which consists of cassava soaked in sugar-cane juice and masticated by women and children. A quantity of this, added to the basic *kachiri* ingredients of manioc, sweet potatoes and water, induces fermentation. *Paiwarri*, which is drunk at feasts in this area, is made from burnt cassavas, boiled manioc juice, boiling water and *kereli*. According to Charles Waterton, who travelled in the Guianas in 1820, the result is 'an abominable ill-tasted and sour kind of fermented liquor'. Many European travellers in South America have had some difficulty in adjusting their palates to local fare!

The second fermentation method involves spreading out damp cassavas on the house-floor with layers of ashes and leaves and leaving them until mould develops. The cassavas are then put in a pot with water and effervescence occurs. The *bernia* of the Orinoco region and the *puchokwa* of the Wai Wai are made in this way.

Chicha may be made from sweet manioc by boiling peeled tubers, mashing them to a pulp, adding sugar if available and leaving them to ferment. The *masato* of the Shipibo Indians in the River Ucayali district of eastern Peru is made in this way.

Manioc drinks are made regularly for home consumption, though they are never drunk with meals. For feasts they are produced in vast quantities, various receptacles being used for the process. Special *paiwarri* troughs, carved and painted and with handles at each end, are known from the Guianas and the Vaupés area; huge earthenware vessels are also widely used (figure 38), with capacities of up to 11 gallons (50 litres) being reported for the Tupinambá of north-east Brazil. If no purpose-built vessel is available, a good canoe may be scrubbed out and used for beer-making. Various wooden stirrers are used (figure 33) and woven mats or fire-fans may be used to cover beer containers. A few days prior to a feast the women of the host village will be fully occupied in making chicha. Wai Wai women making *puchokwa* have to observe certain food taboos; in addition they must not cook or have sexual intercourse during the process.

At feasts chicha is served by women in drinking vessels made from gourds (figure 39), which are passed from hand to hand until they are empty, then promptly refilled. The alcoholic content of manioc beer is not high, only around 2-4 per cent, but as impressive quantities are consumed on these occasions intoxication frequently results.

During a feast, which may last several days, the participants tend not to eat solid food, relying on the nutritive quantities of the chicha to sustain them. As a general rule drinking does not take place at the same time as eating.

38. (Left) Large chicha pot, North-west Amazon or Guyana. (Museum of Mankind, London. Copyright: British Museum.)

39. (Right) Gourd drinking cup, Akawaio Indians, Guyana. (Pitt Rivers Museum, Oxford.)

Other uses of manioc

Manioc has certain other uses besides forming the basis of bread and beer and, in the case of sweet manioc, being a useful vegetable for the pot. In the West Indies and elsewhere, tapioca is used as laundry starch. On a culinary level manioc leaves may be boiled and eaten like spinach: the leaves have a higher protein content than the tubers. The Içá-Japurá tribes, according to Whiffen, boiled manioc leaves, pounded them with a pestle and seasoned them with fish, worms, frogs, ants and peppers. The resulting preparation was consumed with cassava and meat. In the same area, cassava starch was mixed with soaked and pounded tobacco leaves to make a thick dark liquid kept in a gourd and licked from a stick. The Barasana boil an infusion of rotted manioc leaves and thicken it with starch to make a savoury dip; they also use the leaves to blacken the lacquer on gourd vessels.

5
Manioc and daily life

Food

Manioc is the staple crop of many tropical forest Indian groups. It is eaten at every meal and the manioc garden is a much more reliable and stable food source than the hunting expedition. Nevertheless manioc, grown and processed by women, is generally considered a low-status food, whereas the meat and fish procured by men are highly valued. The Wayana say 'there is nothing to eat today' if they only have manioc and no game. While protein is obviously necessary for a well balanced diet to be maintained, the status attached to the hunter is also of considerable significance.

When guests from another village arrive on a visit, they are traditionally offered small quantities of cassava and 'pepper-pot', both manioc products made by women. Usually these are offered by women of the host village to male guests. Among the Wayana this is seen as a symbolic gesture, inviting the male visitors to associate with the marriageable women of the village. Food is intimately connected with the male-female dichotomy in society.

Work

Manioc-processing involves women in a huge amount of labour, especially among groups where cassava is prepared daily, such as the Cubeo, Tatuyo, Barasana and others of the north-west Amazon. Cubeo women have been estimated to spend six to nine hours every day working with manioc. When social events occur, with their concomitant heavy drinking bouts, extra work is involved in preparation of beer by the women of the host village. It is suggested that the chiefs of the Tupinambá married several wives mainly to enable them to cope with the work of providing chicha for their numerous festivals.

In addition to work involving manioc, it should not be forgotten that Indian women have also traditionally coped with fetching water and wood, keeping the house fires going, gathering fruits, nuts and roots in the forest, making pottery (figure 40), looking after children, butchering and cooking game, keeping their houses clean and tidy, and serving their husbands with food and drink at regular intervals. Men, on the other hand, when not engaged in hunting or fishing expeditions, tending their coca plantations, or the occasional bout of house-building or

40. Tiriyo woman making pottery. Surinam. (Copyright: Peter Rivière.)

forest-clearing, frequently have the leisure to relax in their hammocks, sleeping, talking, playing with their children and making the occasional basket (figure 41). While some men will from time to time lend a hand at certain stages of manioc-processing, many consider such work beneath their dignity. The Puinave and Curripaco of the River Inirida in Colombia believe that men's and women's tasks were originally allotted to them by a god.

Trade

Manioc and manioc-related items have always been significant in Amazonian exchange patterns. Trade did not develop merely as a result of contact with Europeans, though this contact has had a dramatic effect on the material culture of the Indians and their way of life. Intertribal trade has always been of great importance, involving quite complex patterns of exchange.

Intertribal trade

Tropical forest Indians were, at least before European contact, largely self-sufficient in terms of their day-to-day requirements.

41. Tiriyo man making a basket. (Copyright: Peter Rivière.)

However, due in many cases to the availability of natural resources, it was easier for some groups than others to produce certain specialist artefacts. Pottery, for example, could only be manufactured in areas where good clay was available; stone-chip manioc graters (figure 42) could only be made if suitable stone was to be found. Groups with access to such materials became very skilled in making artefacts from them. Other items, such as baskets or manioc squeezers, did not depend on the availability of rare materials, but nevertheless certain groups developed an

42. Manioc grater: a valued trade item, Wai Wai Indians, Guyana. (Horniman Museum, London.)

expertise in making them.

Such commodities formed the basis of intertribal trade, resulting in an exchange of specialist products between groups. As well as manioc graters and squeezers, pottery and blow-pipes, trade goods included poisons, hammocks, mats, musical instruments, ceremonial objects, gourd vessels, fish-traps, balls of spun cotton and hunting dogs. Items often travelled great distances from their area of origin, being exchanged a number of times before reaching their final destination.

Intertribal trade should not, however, merely be seen as an exchange of scarce commodities. It is also a means of social interaction between groups, often more important than the actual goods involved. To this end tribes may exchange items they are perfectly well able to produce for themselves, for the purpose of creating and reinforcing social bonds.

European trade

Trade with Europeans began in the sixteenth century when the first explorers came to seek their fortunes in the New World. Many hoped to find wealth in the Amazon comparable to the riches of Peru, highland Colombia and Mexico, and the legend of El Dorado whetted their appetites for gold. In order to provision their expeditions they began to trade with the Indians for cassava and farinha. Sir Walter Raleigh wrote of the cassava he obtained from the Arawaks: 'nothing on earth could have been more welcome to vs next vnto gold, than the great ftore of very excellent bread which we found in thefe *Canoas*, for now our men cried, let vs go on, we care not how farre.'

Gold did not prove to be forthcoming from the Amazon, and the rich cities of legend were never discovered. However, the Europeans found other commodities in the forest which they could exploit, including fine woods, dyestuffs and tobacco, for which they traded with the Indians. From the beginning, metal knives, machetes, axes, fish-hooks and salt were highly prized trade goods, along with less utilitarian items such as beads, combs, cloth, jews' harps and mirrors. These remained popular as time went on, with such items as matches, firearms, soap, sewing-machines, aluminium cooking-pots, radios and outboard motors having been added to the list in more recent years.

Once the colonists had a secure foothold in South America, trading ceased to be a mere matter of amicable exchange. The Europeans developed large sugar plantations and required huge forces of cheap labour to work them. Feuding and the taking of captives had been known from pre-Colombian times in the Amazon and this fact was exploited by the white traders. Certain groups of warlike Indians became involved in 'slave-raiding': the capture of members of weaker groups who were handed over to the Europeans in exchange for trade goods.

Slavery was abolished by the mid nineteenth century, but it was soon replaced under a different guise. In the late nineteenth and early twentieth centuries the 'rubber boom' developed in the Amazon. Thousands of Indian men were employed, often under highly exploitive and cruel conditions, to tap, process and transport wild rubber for white masters. They were provided with trade-goods to create a debt which could only be paid off in disproportionate amounts of rubber. In order to feed their workforces the rubber barons traded with Indian women for large quantities of farinha.

The Amazon boom declined sharply after 1914 due to competition from the new rubber plantations in Malaya and by 1923 it had collapsed. However, rubber extraction has continued on a small scale and in the early 1960s Cubeo women in the Vaupés area of Colombia were contracted to the rubber traders for all the farinha they could produce. They were paid in trinkets which they valued highly, though to our eyes the deal was scarcely a fair one: a pair of cheap ear-rings would be given for twelve baskets of farinha, representing twelve days' labour. Nevertheless, their involvement in the farinha trade has given many Indian women a measure of independence they used not to possess.

Other extractive industries have developed in the Amazon during the twentieth century. The commodities involved include oil, diamonds, bauxite, alluvial gold, paper, brazil nuts, animal skins, tropical fish and cocaine, though the production of this for the drugs trade is strictly unofficial. All of these industries employ Indian labour and therefore create a regular demand for farinha. Their more damaging effects are far-reaching, and will be discussed further in chapter 6.

Intertribal trade and European trade have become part of the same complex network, with Indians trading European goods to each other and also exchanging farinha which eventually ends up in European hands. The more remote tribes may never see a European, but still possess European trade goods. Such goods obviously increase in value the further they travel from their source.

The arrival of the steel axe and the machete have had a

43. Tukano feast. Colombia. (Copyright: B. Moser and D. Tayler Collection.)

remarkable effect on tropical forest horticulture. The axe enables trees to be felled in a fraction of the time taken previously and makes garden clearance a much easier job for men than its stone-bladed predecessor. The machete has revolutionised work for both men and women (figure 4). It can be used for clearing underbrush, for harvesting manioc and other crops, and for peeling tubers and fruits; it is excellent for splitting firewood and butchering game; it is also ideal for cutting reeds and palm-leaves used in basket making and splitting them into suitable widths for plaiting manioc-squeezers, fire-fans, sieves, cassava trays and other baskets. Steel tools are highly prized and when they break the pieces are promptly recycled into smaller implements.

Feasts

Feasts are a frequent occurrence in tropical forest society, and may be held for any number of reasons. Events meriting special celebration include initiation ceremonies, the naming of a child, the cutting of a child's hair, preparation for battle, the clearing of a garden, the harvest of certain crops, convalescence after an illness, and death, to name a few. Certain ceremonies, such as those where the sacred Yurupary musical instruments are displayed, must not be witnessed by women, who may retreat to the rear of the house while they take place. Feasts may also be held spontaneously for no specified reason, serving to promote social cohesion between groups.

The word 'feast' is perhaps a misnomer in our terms, as during these events, which tend to last several days, no solid food is normally consumed. Chicha, frequently manioc beer, provides all the necessary nutrients as well as the desired effect of intoxication. The aim is to drink as much as possible and the guests are provided by their hosts with almost unlimited quantities of beer. The heavy emphasis on hospitality also serves to demonstrate the host's economic standing and the ability of his household to produce a surplus of manioc for festive occasions. Drinking is associated with dancing, singing and the public recital of tribal legends. Traditionally men and women paint elaborate patterns on their bodies for these occasions and the men especially deck themselves in all their finery. Ornaments include feather head-dresses, strings of glass trade-beads and arm and leg bands of stringwork or monkey-fur (figure 43).

When a household head decides to hold a feast, his women folk will be busy for days beforehand preparing chicha (figure 44). Men may join in the work of preparation, but only in a lighthearted manner.

Once the guests have arrived, the host women will serve them with gourds full of chicha, the gourds being passed from hand to hand until they are empty, then promptly refilled. Women join in the dancing and singing, but do not usually become intoxicated. Knowing the effects of alcohol on their men, some women will hide all weapons until the feast is over. Violent quarrels frequently occur under the influence of chicha, and sexual licence is also not uncommon. Intoxication is helped along by the use of coca, tobacco, *yagé* (*Baniopteris caapi*) and other narcotics by the men.

It is customary for the feast to continue until the last drop of beer has been drunk, and it is very bad form for a guest to refuse a drink. If a man cannot consume any more he may, without leaving his seat, disgorge what he has drunk in order to make room for more. From time to time he may clear his head by pouring pepper-juice down his nostrils.

Not surprisingly, in those places where missionaries have been most active, alcoholic beverages and drinking-parties have been frowned on as contrary to Christian ideals. Tribal beliefs and

44. Large chicha pot from the Ucayali River, East Peru. (Museum of Mankind, London. Copyright: British Museum.)

45. Stone *zemi*. Ancient Arawak, Puerto Rico. (Pitt Rivers Museum, Oxford.)

legends have also been suppressed in favour of Christian dogma. As a result feasts are less common and have even been eliminated entirely in some areas. Surplus manioc is made into farinha for trade rather than into chicha for drinking parties.

Beliefs

Amazonian Indians have a complex religious system based on belief in a world of spirits. This spirit world is understood and interpreted by shamans, who often hold considerable power in their communities. Shamans are responsible for curing disease and for communicating tribal myths and legends. Each group has its own legends concerning the origins of manioc and other plants. *Zemies*, the ancient conical stone figures excavated in the West Indies, are said to be representations of the deity who gave manioc to the Arawaks (figure 45).

Specific rites may be performed to promote the continuing abundance of manioc. As there is no particular season at which the tubers are gathered in, it is planting rather than harvesting that tends to be affected by ritual; however, feasts are frequently held at which the whole manioc cycle, from planting right through to consumption, is celebrated in dance and song.

Christine Hugh-Jones (1979) has made an intricate study of the ritual significance of manioc among the Barasana of Colombia and claims that the manioc process may be seen as the female equivalent of the exclusively male Yurupary rites. She draws many interesting parallels between the manioc cycle and the pattern of Barasana life and compares the separation and recombination of the male and female elements of manioc (fibre and starch) with the similar behaviour of the male and female elements in society.

6
Change in Amazonian society

This book has largely been written using the 'ethnographic present' tense to describe traditional ways of life in the Amazonian forest. However, it must be stressed that the situation in which many Indians live today is far removed from the idyll preserved in museum collections and the accounts of early travellers.

The indigenous peoples of South America have suffered centuries of abuse, from the time of the first European contact down to the present day. The gold-hungry *conquistadores* drove them from their traditional lands, subjected them to slavery and introduced smallpox and other diseases which ravaged whole populations. Resistance to infection is low even today and, while missionaries have brought medical aid to the Indians, the diseases they are curing are frequently European imports.

The role of the missionaries is open to debate, and their treatment of the Indians has varied enormously. On the one hand, besides Christianity, useful trade-goods and medical support, the Jesuits, Catholics, protestants and evangelists have brought education to people who were living in a rapidly developing continent without its benefits. On the other hand they have in many cases discouraged tribal customs and beliefs and introduced a set of moral values foreign to the environment in which they have been planted. The decline of the chicha feast is just one example of the loss of a significant social institution. Another is the disappearance of the communal house as Indians are encouraged to live in nuclear families.

Some Indian groups were sedentary before contact; others have become so as a result of it, settling close to the material benefits of towns, mission-stations and trading posts. This has introduced them to the white man's economy and created a dependence on his goods; it can also lead to increased manioc production, which helps to pay for them. The traditional ideals of sharing food and belongings are being eroded in favour of Western-style acquisitiveness. In their eagerness to possess European goods, many Indians find themselves inextricably in debt to their white employers.

Work itself is no longer just a matter of hunting, gathering, collecting and gardening for subsistence. Indian men are increasingly employed in the various extractive industries, helping to exhaust the environment which traditionally provided them with a livelihood. Deforestation for roads and ranches contributes to the destruction of the tropical forest, and hydro-electric projects result in the flooding of large areas previously used for cultivation. Even manioc, once it becomes a cash-crop, exerts unprecedented pressure on the available land. The reduction of the forest means that men must travel further and further to hunt. As more and more manioc is consumed in lieu of meat or fish, protein deficiency diseases are developing.

Some Indian groups have become resigned to change, and some indeed approve of it. Many, however, are still determined to maintain their traditional ways of life without interference; but their tribal lands are being encroached upon and few politicians are sympathetic to their cause. There is little consultation at the planning stages of extractive projects. Even where Indian reservations have been created, such as the Xingu Indian Park in Brazil, they are vulnerable to invasion and exploitation.

In the face of these problems, manioc still survives as a staple crop and the methods of cultivating and processing it remain little changed for the time being. It remains the major occupation and preoccupation of Indian women: not merely a food but a way of life. Cassava and chicha, while the tropical forest still exists, may prove to be among its most durable products.

7
Museums to visit

While all the following institutions hold manioc-related material in their collections, it may not be on permanent display. Visitors are advised to telephone and check on displays to avoid disappointment.

Cambridge University Museum of Archaeology and Anthropology, Downing Street, Cambridge CB2 3DZ. Telephone: 0223 337733 or 333516.

City of Bristol Museum and Art Gallery, Queen's Road, Bristol, Avon BS8 1RL. Telephone: 0272 222000. Material in store may be viewed by appointment.

Commonwealth Institute, Kensington High Street, London W8 6NQ. Telephone: 01-603 4535.

Hancock Museum, Barras Bridge, Newcastle upon Tyne, Tyne and Wear NE2 4PT. Telephone: 091 232 2359.

Horniman Museum, London Road, Forest Hill, London SE23 3PQ. Telephone: 01-699 1872, 2339 or 4911.

Museum of Mankind (The Ethnography Department of the British Museum), 6 Burlington Gardens, London W1X 2EX. Telephone: 01-686 1555.

Pitt Rivers Museum, South Parks Road, Oxford OX1 3PP. Telephone: 0865 270927.

Saffron Walden Museum, Museum Street, Saffron Walden, Essex CB10 1JL. Telephone: 0799 22494.

8
Further reading

Some of these works are out of print and will only be available through libraries.

Carmichael, E.; Hugh-Jones, S.; Moser, B. and Tayler, D. *The Hidden Peoples of the Amazon*. British Museum Publications, 1985.

Dole, G. E. 'Techniques of Preparing Manioc Flour as a Key to Culture History in Tropical America' in A. Wallace (editor), *Men and Cultures: Selected Papers of the Fifth International Congress of Anthropological and Ethnological Sciences*, 1960, 241-8.

Goldman, I. *The Cubeo*. Illinois Studies in Anthropology 2, 1963.

Hames, R. B., and Vickers, W. T. *Adaptive Responses of Native Amazonians*. Academic Press, 1983.

Hugh-Jones, C. *From the Milk River*. Cambridge University Press, 1979.

Koch-Grünberg, T. *Zwei Jahre unter den Indianern*. Ernst Wasmuth, 1909.

Lathrap, D. W. *The Upper Amazon*. Thames and Hudson, 1970.

Murphy, Y. and R. F. *Women of the Forest*. Columbia University Press, 1974.

Musée d'Ethnographie, Geneva. *La Marmite Wayana*. Geneva, 1979.

Olsen, F. *On the Trail of the Arawaks*. University of Oklahoma Press, 1974.

Oviedo y Valdes, G. F. de. *Historia General y Natural de las Indias, Islas y Tierra-firme del Mar Oceano*. D. José Amador de los Rios (editor). Real Academia de la Historia, Madrid, 1851-5.

Raleigh, Sir Walter. *The Discouerie of the Large, Rich, and Bewtiful Empyre of Guiana*. Scolar Press, 1967.

Rivière, P. 'Of Women, Men and Manioc', *Etnologista Studier* 38, Goteborgs Etnografiska Museum, 1987, 178-201.

Roosevelt, A. C. *Parmana — Prehistoric Maize and Manioc Subsistence along the Amazon and Orinoco*. Academic Press, 1980.

Roth, W. E. *An Introductory Study of the Arts, Crafts and Customs of the Guiana Indians*. 38th Annual Report of the Bureau of American Ethnology, Smithsonian Institution, Washington, 1924.

Steward, J. H. (editor). *Handbook of South American Indians,* volume III. Bureau of American Ethnology, Smithsonian Institution, Washington, 1948.

Survival International Review. An annual publication concerned with the survival of threatened indigenous groups in Third World countries.

Wallace, A. R. *A Narrative of Travels on the Amazon and Rio Negro.* Ward Lock, 1889.

Waterton, Charles. *Wanderings in South America.* Century Publishing, 1984.

Whiffen, T. *The North-West Amazons,* Constable, 1915.

Yde, J. *Material Culture of the Wai Wai.* National Museum of Copenhagen, Etnografisk Roekke X, 1965.

INDEX

Page numbers in italic refer to illustrations